To
FLOSSIE LEWIS,
LEE SAMUEL,
and
PAUL HELLER,
who
willingly
offer
their
expertise
whenever
I
cry
for
help.

A PaperStar Book, published in 1998 by Penguin Putnam Books for
Young Readers, 345 Hudson Street, New York, NY 10014.
PaperStar is a registered trademark of The Putnam Berkley Group, Inc.
The PaperStar logo is a trademark of The Putnam Berkley Group, Inc.
Originally published in 1991 by Grosset & Dunlap.
Published simultaneously in Canada
Manufactured in China
Library of Congress Catalog Card Number: 91-70668
ISBN 978-0-698-11663-4

19 20 18

RUTH HELLER
WORLD OF LANGUAGE

UP, UP AND AWAY

A Book About Adverbs

Written and illustrated by

RUTH HELLER

Penguin Putnam Books for Young Readers

ADVERBS work terrifically
when answering specifically…
"How?"
"How often?"
"When?"
and "Where?"

Penguins all dress
DECENTLY.

Toe
dancers
practice
FREQUENTLY.

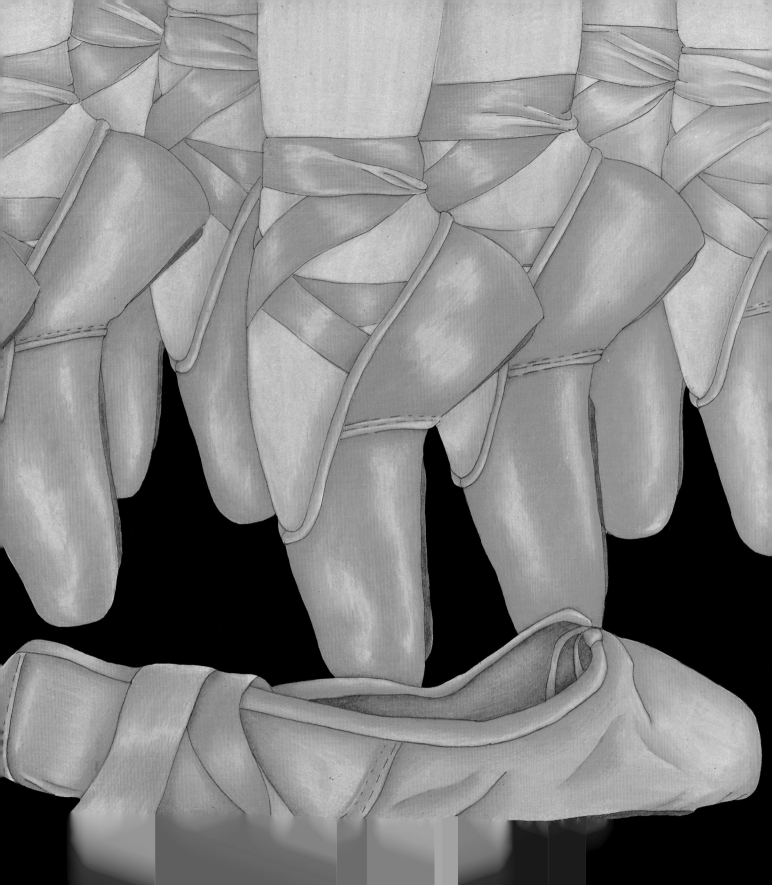

This house was painted RECENTLY...and

small green frogs
live
THERE.

Before an ADVERB
answers "When?"
it always
answers
"Where?"

This ship will sail
AWAY
TODAY.

It will not sail
TODAY
AWAY.

ADVERBS
work terrifically
when asking
most specifically,
"When?"
and
"How?"
and
"Where?"
and
"Why?"

WHEN
do
owls
hoot?

HOW do you do?

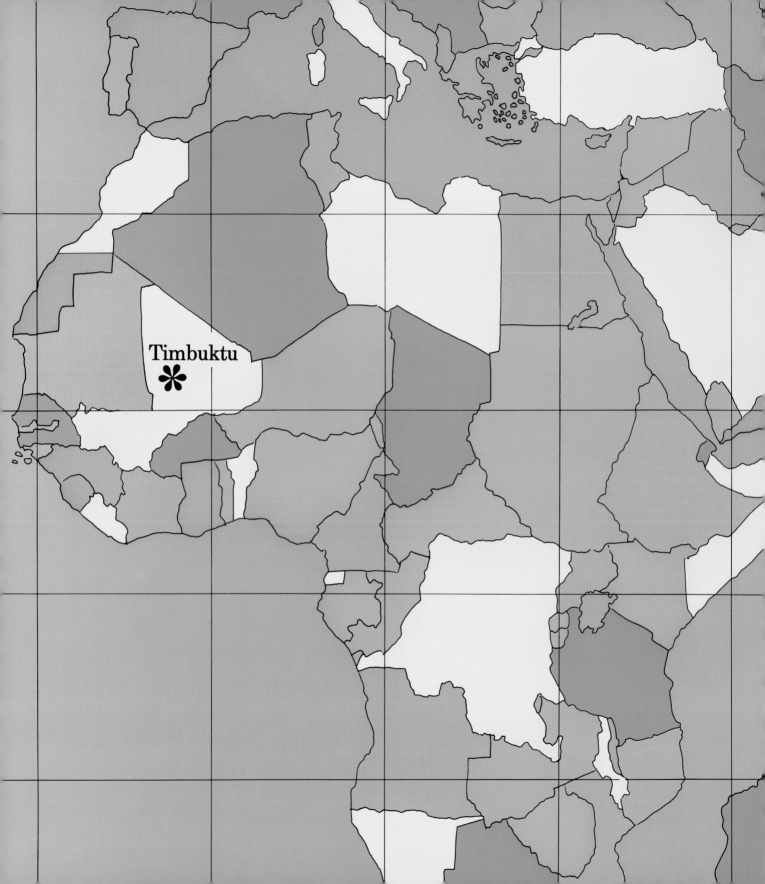

Timbuktu

WHERE
in the world
is
Timbuktu?

And
WHY
do
pandas
eat
bamboo?

Some ADVERBS tell to what extent…

This cat is RATHER corpulent,
and VERY soft and purry.
She seems EXTREMELY
confident and MORE than
SOMEWHAT furry.
She's TOO well fed,
this SO well-bred,
ornamental
quadruped.

I REALLY wish she would not shed.

My eyes become QUITE blurry.

Many
ADVERBS
end
in
LY
(pronounced
to
rhyme
with
bumblebee).

GENTLY
rub
this
lamp
and
see
genies
show
up
MAGICALLY.

Hot-air balloons drift
DREAMILY, and REGALLY they rise.

Some
ADVERBS
end
in
WARD,
and
others
end
in
WISE...
BACKWARD..

LIKEWISE...COUNTERCLOCKWISE.

To recognize an ADVERB,
sometimes you must be clever,
because it may be positive
like YES, INDEED,
FOREVER...

or it may be negative like
NO
and **NOT**
and **NEVER**.

NO, I have **NOT**
seen a purple cow.
I NEVER
hope to see one.

But I can tell you
anyhow...
I'd rather see
than be one.

Are you aware that when ADVERBS compare,
all of them use LESS and LEAST?
One-syllable ADVERBS, you've probably guessed,
also compare
with an
ER
or an
EST...

SOON

SOONER

SOONEST

LESS SOON

LEAST SOON

All of
these
clocks will be striking at noon.

Please don't be confused.
MORE and MOST must be used with ADVERBS ending in LY.

Snails slither
SLOWLY
at a
snail's pace…

MORE
SLOWLY,

MOST
SLOWLY,
this snail   lost the race.

LESS SLOWLY,

LEAST SLOWLY,
this one's in first place.

IRREGULAR ADVERBS
are usually strange
because when comparing
they totally change.

Victor

friend
cat
chiken
flower
skool

Victor spells BADLY,

Shalina

friend
cat
chicpin
flowr
school

Shalina spells WORSE.

Andrew
frend
kat
chikn
flowr
sckool

And Andrew is
ursed. Andrew
spells
WORST.

José
friend
cat
chicken
flower
school

**LEAST
BADLY**
José.

José gets
an A.

Becky
freind
cat
chicken
flower
school

**LESS
BADLY**
spells Becky,

When
comparing
two things,
like these creatures with wings,
you must use
the
COMPARATIVE
FORM.

Of these two
egrets that
you
see...

this
one

arrived
MORE recently.

To
compare
more
than two,
this is what
you must do:
You must use the
SUPERLATIVE
FORM.
Of
all
these
creatures
in the
sea…
this one

arrived
MOST
RECENTLY.

Don't ever use
NOT and **NEVER**
together.
Don't say
"We don't never have fun"
because
you'll be using two negatives,
and
you need to be using
just one.

You
will
always
be in trouble
if
your
negatives
are
double!